T0208226

RHYTHMS OF LIFE

Victor Okam

iUniverse, Inc.
Bloomington

iUniverse books may be ordered through booksellers or by contacting:

iUniverse
1663 Liberty Drive
Bloomington, IN 47403
www.iuniverse.com
1-800-Authors (1-800-288-4677)

Because of the dynamic nature of the Internet, any web addresses or links contained in this book may have changed since publication and may no longer be valid. The views expressed in this work are solely those of the author and do not necessarily reflect the views of the publisher, and the publisher hereby disclaims any responsibility for them.

Any people depicted in stock imagery provided by Thinkstock are models, and such images are being used for illustrative purposes only.

Certain stock imagery © Thinkstock.

ISBN: 978-1-4502-9581-9 (sc)
ISBN: 978-1-4502-9580-2 (ebook)

Printed in the United States of America

iUniverse rev. date: 02/22/2011

CONTENTS

DEDICATION

To my Mother and my Father who interred
this seed but are not here to see it sprout

Acknowledgement

A very deep thank you to Eberekpe Whyte, a
wonderful guy who loves success and would want to
share it, Endy Amadi, Godwin Amaefula for their
support and my lecturer, Professor Isidore Diala

THE FLAME

Shines bright and sweet at full strength
Spreading its glory to vistas far and wide
Alluring, warm, cosy, involving all the senses
Desire peaks, nearing optimal contentment,
Then slowly fades the sparks.

It comes alive in shimmering glow.
The heart awakes to duty
Half energy, indifferent;
The hearth, cold, full of ash;
Lonely anthill, forlorn, drab;
Faith lacks continuity.

The flicker appears in renewed form.
Sanguine spirit springs life,
Full mobility, aspiration cracks the brain.
Body, full of vigour and pomp
Dance the samba of change-
Heightened piano, allegro, adagio
Abrupt crescendo; emotions turn pale
The blood chills, the heart broods.

Melancholy reborn
Ash spreads on spectacle,
The energetic gyre shrinks,
Confusion. Forms distorted, smoke spirals
From the ruins of splendour
Gentle wind fans the aftermath of life;
The flame blazes no more.
Profound silence reigns.

BREATHE

Wind-tossed leaf
That lands on unknown destinations
A chameleon that alters when changes call.
It separates us from optimal realisations
It gives joy and shrouds us with grief
When we most desire its course.

Like the bees' comb,
At dawn, it proffers tasty liquid;
At noon, the liquid drops with dregs;
Taste turns sour at dust.
Yet it is the nectar every bird covets.

This unholy halo lightens existence.
It derails senses that dare its mystery
And abandons mortals in various ashes
When years of yore are recalled.

This puzzle builds and pulls down
As we yearn for its glossy deceit
That ridicules the strength of our knowledge.

THE DAWN HAS COME

The dawn has come,
Let every mortal rise
To the demands of existence
To the hopes and aspirations
That validate the nature of vanity

The dawn has come
The shine slumbers no more
As human lots glow in it.

The dawn has come
The clouds wander aimlessly
Like the entreating eyes that stare at them-
For succour and respite
Which are no where in the mass.

The dawn has come
Soon the threatening twilight will arrive
With awaiting darkness to offer its trauma
That set hope on flight.

The dawn has come
Let every strength that struggles
Know foretime that those broils
Have no life-giving victual
But bitter waters that trouble
Spirit, soul and body.

FORTITUDE

I am nature's sample of ridicule
Bodies convulse with laughter
As they behold me.
Joyful tears cascade cheeks
As they mock my state-
They know well the cause of their humour;
They have witnessed the vanity of efforts;
They recognise him who is the prey
A condemned dormant receiver.

The game of duck and drake
Completes the rounds of mirth,
But as I am skipped along,
I dwell with no appreciator.

This head has played host to countless fears;
As the lion's heart turns pigeon liver,
The brave bears the convergence
Of sleight antelopes
And calls to recess inactive paws.

The dawn has come;
Can the sun arise?
The carcass no more hosts flies and revels
Because the fetid oil is dried-
Even fossilization beckons
Aaaah...life has played hide and seek with me.
Like the forlorn child,
My bleary eyes stare at the mocking heaven
The boa that swallows a prey
Must not scale a distance,
Fate so brutish! Divorce me not
Let's wear along this path.

ORPHAN

The cast of the world has informed this vacancy.
Daily the burden of Calvary cross
Stands at the pathway of activities.

Dumb to tell the tale of parental exit;
As the beauty was unknown.
Her warm bosom, buried in dreams.
As she resides in earth`s womb.

This heart lacks the fire of continuity
The liver bows to ever-imposing horror
What utters groans,
Shares affinity with death.

Surely the orchestrating child at the bush path
Heeds the mystery of unseen drums.
But fate's wanton whacks
Are the forbidden tune
That plagues the desire to share a dance.

Better dissolve with space
And be welcomed in starry realm
Than tread twice this awful passage.

WAILING

Accursed be the desire
That reduced us thus!
Here we satisfy the ambitions of grim hearts.
The stares of bizarre killers
Spell the imminence of assured danger.

But earth cannot hide
From the scourging shine
Nor cease to protest with cracks.
In shackles and fetters the downcast gasp
Embracing in isolation the rhythms of clangs-
Companions of our wretched state.
Calm cauldrons, menacing chains, hoisted irons,
Are determiners of our destiny,
If not laid at the altars of avid gods,
We are transferred to white hands as barters.
As we yield gains that bring us sorrow,
In agony, we bear the burden that breaks us
And seek redemption in Heaven's mandate.

Oh merciless bullies!
Our howls, the bleeding rings of our wrists,
Our rabid skulls- even our cooperate grieves
Testify that innocence is stifled without cause.

Though this stead seem our eternity,
We call upon threatening death
To waste no more its tricks on our beings,
But swiftly come and hurl us
To the abode where the face of existence
Without mortals radiate glory.

NOMADES

Cylindal shanties gap
One another in shrubby hectares
Eyes crane to behold lively human forms
That are part of our globe.

Almost lost to solitude
They do not envy human concerns
Nor desire the cosmetics that give us form
But are happy in their proud aloneness.

Seasons come and go with attendant odds
Yet like the unravished gold,
They remained neither waning nor ceasing.

The ancient mountains, cliffs, valleys, and vegetations
Know and welcome them as compatriots
While we, in vain glory, battle nature
Alas! They re-enact biological custom-
Procreating, sucking, giving sucks, sleeping, waking,
Yet without our sterile anxiety and covetousness.

They know the peace that nature offers.
They negate deception;
With their herds, gains, pride and continuity
Come as balm to bloody wound.

The fellowship of their herd
Makes them oblivious of humans
While we throttle pillar to post to acquire tinsels
And in futility the spectacle fades
As the rainbow rolls heavenward.

ASPIRATION

All we ask for
Is for the fingers that go
To the mouth to have enough strength
To return to the bowel.

We do not ask for conditioners of air
As our being knows well the taste of cold;
We have no need for refrigerators
For we have not extra to preserve.

All we ask for
Is for our lone thatches
To have dwelling places
Even among groves, slums
And evading floods.

We do not covet flats and duplexes
As we know that the death of Maroko
Gives birth to the city of comfort
As evacuation is a prerequisite for acquisition.
And revenue-yielding shacks
Must be bulldozed as ordered
For the metropolis to be magnificent.
While we reside under tree shades
Or end wherever blustering rain places us.

All we ask for
Are those vehicles
Where our backs will back the front
As we wear happily along
The terrific jammed routes.

We do not demand the exotic automobiles that snake
Meander, and aerodynamise the crammed motorways
With awakening and deafening blares.

We have never asked for escorts and guards
For we are friends of all
And no skeleton breathes in our cupboard.
All we ask for is that the eagles
Gliding unattainable heights
Should know it was earth
That launched them to their position.

EXPEDITION

The dogs have gone into the forest,
The hunters hang their guns and search lights
The presence of the dogs will surely
Bring drought of excreta in the bush

Akpankolo kpankolo
 Akpankolo kpankolo
 Udu m o, ogene
 Udu m o, ogene
 Onye o mara
 Suru ya ya ya
 Suru yaa...

The hunters' bags are full
The siblings of the preys are in ash
They wear caution like the nervous chicks;
Treach of bereftment has reduced us thus
While their pride weighs down their shoulders.

 Akpankolo kpankolo
 Akpankolo kpankolo
 Udu m o, ogene
 Udu m o, ogene...

The glorious gyre widens
The belly is tumid;
The cheeks fat up;
Noisy laughters rent the air...
Feet of the hunters wobble
Because the rainbow is fading
Suru ya ya ya lurks by.

The burden of spoil, moans of the spoiled
And fear of the future foil the hunters' hope.
Their paths are foggy
They grapple for sight and breath
The once elegant looks are rumpled
The flapping leaves have graced baseness
Suru ya ya ya heightens its tempo.

Akp-an-ko-lo…kpan-n-ko-lo a-kpan-kolo kpan-kolo
a-kpan-kolo kpa...
The tongues have cleft to the roof of mouth;
The vultures that fart will never
Harvest applause!

Onye o mara
 Suru ya ya ya
Suru yaaa!
Yes! suru ya ya ya is the fate of all predators
It ushers the bolt of the Almighty
Halting errant feet when tom-toms die away.
They are deflated and out
Because they profane the sanctity
Of the land… and of the game too.

Let not the stealthy rat deliberately
Chew the medicine man's bag!
And let not the medicine man
Roast its mouth.

Akpankolo kpankolo...
The isolated spoilers are back!
Never mind, Suru ya ya ya awaits them.

TRAILINGS

Sacrifice does not kill a junction
The dust bin can not be famished;
No matter how the arse is cleansed
On it must stick the stench of diarrhoea.

The fellowship of the egret on herds
Is a demonstration of the cow's debt to it.
The heads that stir the hornet must
Bear the pain of countless stings.

The kite, the kite is gliding
Let every chick be vigilant
The kite, the kite is gliding
Swooping abides in those wings.

Let quacking gather in the hen's breast
For those that have offspring
Harvest the field of grief.

THE CHASE

The chase,
The chase is hot
Let the high and the low seek shelter.

The chase,
The chase hedges us about
To show that the water will consume
One foot where it drowned the other.

The chase
The chase warns us
That the grasshopper devoured by okpoko is deaf

The chase
The chase is the divine providence-
No matter how the feet run
Upon the smith's forge and kiln will
All steel be fired and beaten to shape.

DECEPTION

The beauty of the rose is its thorn
It has left my fingers bloody
But like dawn, I hate to retreat
Until I nip this bud.

The rose breeds thorn and dares callers
And thorn is rose and rosy
But is the rose thorn?

Yes!
They appear in varied camouflage
The red is the danger signal;
The pink is the traditional grace
The white is all that glitters which is not
This lures explorers and resolutes.

But colours are rose and rosy
Also are thorns and thorny.
They decoy with comeliness.
Like the melody of the parrot's tongue,
They invite us to their world
But as the tiger spider,
They ensnare us with their charm
And dump us in various ruins;
Imprisoned prey can merely writhe.
The nature of the rose is
The way of existence.

DESTINY

A day will come
When the body will still
When vale of tears will not upturn inevitability
When sterility will cast grim halo
On erstwhile fist and wit.

A day will come
This day not distant.
When all will desire my alliance
When splendours of life
Will become fairy tale
As all that made a man
Will have life in epitaph.

A day will come
So near I feel.
When worms will convocate
And revel on this flesh
Asserting our mutual fraternity.

A day will come
True indeed!
When virtue will desert the numb skull
While in lone ness, the bare bones
Await the exploit of prowling termites.

How we will dance home
Is anonymous to mortals;
Through water, land, and or sea-
The wit in vain hazards guess
As the tempo beckons daily.

Defiant to our perplexity,
The hunter's nozzle awaits the prey.
I fret not at this;
As it is our collective destiny.

RHYTHM OF ISOLATION

Antiquities of thatches mourn in ruinous heap
Hearths are dry and cold;
Crow are on exile
Silence guards the lone debris of eaves;
Even earthen moulds exist in broken ranks
Lending easeful passage to rain.

Lardens are no more;
Rodents and pests fold their arms
And gaze in forlorn expectation.

Famished ants file out their complains
As maniac termites scramble for rotten boughs,
Habitation in pool of hue awry
Beckons the straying broom.

Earth renders her grief
As fallen leaves deprive her
Soothe of wind and rain;
While the chirp of birds pierce the air
Pronouncing their desire to soar.

From the four winds, bloom is born
Abandoning former ranks in novel stead.
As filth embraces tidiness,
Reconstruction brings warmth,
Crows bask in renewed duty;
Night divorces darkness and
Accommodates the moon and stars
To cheer the stir of optimism.
Activities permeate loneliness
Mortality is the sport of nature.

NIGHT CHILD

Night child
Is he who knows well every chink
That visits the alms' bowl
Whose sheen skin bears the wrath
Of the searing shine.

Night child
Is he whom nature
Blessed with boundless greenery
But who is a great amazement of beings
Sorriest of soiled sorts.

Night child
Hosts hordes of avid flies
When wars proffer droughts and famines.
He feels and knows winter in summer
When cruel leaders sport
Reduce him to a refugee and a destitute.

Night child
Are those sulky eyes, charred skins, vim less ribs,
That illustrate lack and desolation.
As the bowel retreats to the spine,
Those entreating eyes keep vigil with hopelessness.

Night child
Also is he whom He formed as others
Who knew the warmth of gestation and birth
But whose sole sin is to share existence
Where insatient, inhuman predators romp.

VOICE OF THE ALMAGERIS

This realm, they crowd with us;
With no mean tending, we graduate to unsafe teens
Roaming street corners and garbage heaps
Yet haste cannot overtake the shadow;
We survive via passer-by largesse
Still they call us folks.

We are compatriots only in principle
And when faith's obligations summon us to duty,
We brandish deadly sabres, arrows, spear,
As we fulfil cause and purpose.
But when the tide ebbs,
We become the debris that litter crannies

We ask: must we remain the whetstone
That makes blades sharp?
Must we be the scum that covers
The natural taste of wine?
Must we remain qualifiers of debasement?
And swell the circle of servitude

We desire translation
We deserve supposed essence
Or isolation in life other world

MAD MAN

Am made than mad
In solitude, my being is unique with contentment
My monody unresolved puzzle
That disquiets artless minds.

In tranquil forge, I fabricate thoughts
Which sages have and treasure;
Like the spider's craft, my attire shines
Summoning awful sights to its beauty.
I entertain you with amusement and dread;
You meddle and trouble my peace.
I embrace oddities, while vigilance is your bane
You fail to comprehend all
Are churned by identical tempest.

I befriend the world's recklessness
While your concern can not
Undo my profound engagement
I mesh with night and explore its mystery;
You fear and shudder at it presence.

Ignorant of our mutual fraternity
You bemuse me with your thought of superiority
Realising not that all foreheads
Are bare to space-
Pre-eminence and modesty are imaginative trifles.

Only ranks betray us with pride of place
No lizard possesses the grip that rounds the trunk
We are all prostrate with measures of belly aches.

SLEEP

Unpredicted eclipse of consciousness
Your exploit scores premium on dead man's eyes
Yet you waste duty on watch man's sight
Defying mortal knowledge,
You call and depart at will.
The bravest and the weakest are your twin victims.

In you, dreams unfold ambitions
Establishing happy moments of goals
When wakefulness separates
Your plastic glories dissolve.
Abandoning the body in regrets,
In vain the eyes covet your visitation;
Unable to crack your code,
Flesh remains a mere porter that
Holds watch for nature.

CONSTERNATION

The plagues of this stead
The drones of these gongs
Warp me to the faraway piano I hear
It thrills with fabulous tunes
Like fish to the wriggling worm;
I make for the melody.

I sail on the wing of the wind;
In the attendant storms
I squirm at breezy cold
The head with chattering teeth ponders this rumba
While the rumbling sea mocks my fickleness
Assuring the air-borne cotton damp at its surface.

In this isle,
New amazements void teeming expectation
The hunger that brought me here
Lacks fulfilment of desire.
As the betrayed feel the weight of delusion, the
Prodigal reflects on the samba call.

Heeding, the gongs bring back the
Thrills and vision of loathed glory.
The grasses have same green in all kingdoms
The disgruntled egret at the cattle's back
Knows the vanity of avidity;
The prize of dreams is abrupt awakening.

WATERSHED

Bother not about life
Nor care about the burden of death.

If in both, self is stuffed with
Countless grief, anguish, isolation,
We are not better than the Alps.

When in life,
We host countless upheavals,
Pray often the relief of death,
Yet unyielding it forbids us.

When alive, happy moments of extreme bliss
Conspire with cruel interludes of pain
To baulk flesh and blood;
Survival becomes routine rat race,
Zeal of continuity constantly is
Faced with vagueness
Puissant wits groan and mourn
The treach of this watershed.
Humanity is but a preserved course of fate.

ALIENATION

The eagles have eaten dung.
The height of gliding is deserted
The mountains house no more the eagle's egg
Because the hind wings
Lack strength to attain altitudes.
Predators disdain the glory of peaks
Because the wind judges their acts
And make their poor-pose(s)
Wasteful dispositions.

What heaven magnets,
Must grace the earth!

Rebirth.
The eagles have gone on penance:
Corrupt feathers are shed
Cold has pined the dare flesh
Reprove begets obedience!
The warmth of fresh feathers
Brings back the vigour of wings.
Fresh glides defy storms
The glory of duty is back.

I am transported back to my bedrock
My rock, my stead, my home.

OLD WOMAN

Erstwhile fleshy beauties
Lie straight on wrinkled bony chest
Those sags were once succulent
Exploits of thirsty sucks
Denied them of traditional dance.
As the cheeks slap the mouth,
Charred ivories in interstice rest.
As frowning belly bemoans
The drought of proofs of ovulation,
Plump thighs shrink and dry vaginal moist;
Shunning coital jerks as conception has fled.

As elegant gaits and flaunting arse wobble
Walk sticks come to the rescue.
Light of reason flickers away;
As imbecility enthrones itself
Reducing bride price to awful investment.

Like chaffs, buxomness haplessly
Seek asylum in spin-stars.
Cosmetic daubing and brisk smiles
Form array of wrinkles.
Costumes are but mere worn rags...
The rhythm of this passage
Cows my craving to set sail.

ASCENSION

The castrated hyena in full fury
Can not alter night's quietude.
The venom-filled adder its poison
Drained upon the tortoise shell
Shall reap frustration and despair
As it returns to its dust licking.

Let the ass bray at no grass
Let the ox low at the absence of fodder
Let the range hen chirm at the hawk's swoop...

As the spiral smoke mesh with the cloud,
Mortality is the gliding cumulus
Whose strength knows no steadfastness
But dispersion as threatening wind comes.

Like the faith of the excited turgid phallus
At the sight of alluring female genital,
We yearn for the exploration of all vistas;
And like the weary phallus`s retreat to its sheath
At the end of coitus
We welter in mortal dispositions.

Ascension is the reserve
Of immortality.

LOVE

Ugly rainbow that ascends
With all its comely fortune!
Like the queer glint, you dapple glory
On passionate hearts.
And abandon them in impromptu darkness.

You befool disciples
When your wiles score premium on their skills.
There is no muse trait in you
Half-blind god, arched with deceitful arrows.

Nakedness spells innocence, chastity, loyalty,
But when you appear,
You negate the subtle nature of this form.

You spread illusions of beauty on your devotees;
Turning them blind, you abscond
And leave them broken hearted.
Yet they like the Phoenix,
Hope to resurrect from your spoil.

I enthrone hearts that despise you.
With the seaman's anchor
I hold their unyeildedness against
Your luring tempest
O purblind, war drunk, juvenile deity
Who sail without compass
And berth at bland minds' shore.

Where is love?
Save that isolation on the graceful cross.
Where innocence was nailed for redemption.
In Him abides no frail wings,
Nor deceitful nakedness and half sight
That led to mismatch.
He has neither vile quivers nor lethal arrows
Which pin passion to their stake.
But with spread invitation
He beckons all too eternal bliss.

VAINGATHERERS

Where are those whose
Mouths turn Holy Book
To inglorious self- praise?
They have turned Heaven's purpose
To empires of selfish aggrandisement.

They are auctioneers of holy gifts
Making the reek of mints
Prerequisite of altar positions;
While givers of mite gain
Reference only on gospel's pages.

In this grasping trade,
Only marked givers receive
Their palms of blessing
Which are replete with vile gloss
That goes as it came
While receivers are left in delusion.

You who con others
In the hopes of glory
Whilst you are sample of lack,
Enrich yourself before bathing
Others in rivers of affliction and bondage.

You neither lead nor follow
Divine writ- the way to eternal bliss.
You only gather what your tongue sows.
In another's vineyard.

The master of the field will soon come
He that winnows will appear with his fork
And hurl you to eternal scourge.

FEMINISM

The ostriches and the peacocks
Flaunt their colours.
They equip themselves with different arguments
To fight their God-given rights.
From across realms
They holler for empowerment.
But who is denied what?

Those who demand equality
Are quite the brambles that sprout
Among shrubs and prick at will.
They are the spread who give
Colour and taste to daily bread.
Yet they accuse the teeth of biting hard.
Like the sick, they must be carried
To distant infirmary where they dictate to the physician
Appropriate medication.

The air has blown,
The hen's breast is uncovered.
Teachers and preachers of empowerment,
Happiness overwhelms you in your matrimony
But other folks must kemp for equality with their hussies?

You who teach enthronement to rural folk,
Don't you shiver when your pairs roar
For your home to know peace?
But they should fight their husbands
To assert your bias.

You and we know true feminism:
To visit the widows and the barren,
To emancipate your harem-caged folks,
To allow rural folk space in your elitist trips,
To make them know the beauty of life,
Instead of carting away their bumper harvests.

I deny not the status of the lioness;
For the lion comes from her womb.
But let the bereft
Cry only when they are deprived.

HOLLOWNESS

He who is cured of ibi
And he accommodates swollen stomach
Should be left to go
To the spirit land and relish
The course he avidly wants.
Our state is like the air-filled bag;
When punctured, fatness is reduced to worthless rag.
When things that make a nation
Demand our attention,
Giant hood wears the cloak of falsehood
And feign blindness to responsibilities.

Like the defeated nza
We covet modesty.
But fail to realise that humility
Proffers the strength that breeds giants.
Let not the burning cricket think
Its drilling oil is testimony of affluence,
But mere waste of essence
A vague glory.

AFTERMATH

They have swallowed the pestle
And must sleep standing erect

They have stillbirths
Because their eggs
Were fertilized by
Diseased semen.

He who hops from the ground
To the anthill
Is still on the earth
The can not be faster than their shadows
The claws of justice are at destinations
The make times in jail
Because the spirits witness their base affluence.
Got via the peoples' resources.

Falsified ledgers, pen-robbery, bloated contract fees,
Laundered wealth, slug- speed national plannings,
Negligence of duties, looting of treasuries,

Are the mire that must
Stick on our feet and clog haste.

THAT COUNTRY

That country which negates humanity
Which glorifies mediocrity to giant hood
Where drunken monkeys gambol,
In that country, romping elephants
Grab every greenery on their path
Altering rules and orders to suit their recklessness

Like angry locusts,
They swarm the crude-rich field.
That country where leftists have rights;
Where boot men recycle civil rule
And sourly swoop on parrots
When they want to voice out correctness.

Where chicks are forced to shelter
When they gather their ranged lots;
Where a missing ship load of crude
Comes back gracefully;
Its content vanished by the sun
And is amiably welcomed like a prodigal
Is where life is eked.

Where I come from is a contrast:
Of filth and flamboyance,
Of black and bleak hearts.
Where many share abodes with lunatics
While few in towering edifices climb heavenward.

Some grace life in pigs' slums
While few in velvet beddings snore;
Lots are eating with rats
No! They eat rats as food
While edible chunks exude life in bins.

In this country, national wealth
Is the birthright of a few;
Yet lots exist on the brink of lack.
They adorn priceless agbadas, asokes, abadas,
While their compatriots in rags trail on.

That country is in dusk;
Still slumbering,
While others had embraced dawn with shine.

AWFUL PATH

The path of our leaders is twilight,
Toilers are caught in its attendant darkness.

The path of our leaders is thorny
When civil feet tread unauthorized.

The path of our leaders is full of honey
When pens and swagger sticks stir the comb.

The honey of leadership turns sour
When the ruled contest the straightness of lines.

Those cloned in their form carry along
And manifest the true nature of zombies.

The path of our leaders is full of gidigwom
Because they fill the stage with cacophonies
Whose tunes civil hearts dread to hear.

This rumba is a reserve of the initiates;
Which fades in a labyrinth mistune.
The ways of leadership shimmer hopeless gloss
That lures to despair.

SOUL-JEERS

Stop! Go; Come; Halt! At-Ten-Shun!
This; That; Yes; No...
This is the tradition of this industry.
Opposites define their nature
Killing and maiming is their badge of rank
Zombism is the streptococcus
That poisons their humane blood.

They are the human nightmares
Usurping at will; but hate to be removed.
They put to comatose any genuine course
And parade their masquerade,
Which loathes civil-aliens.

Like burr, they stick to our being
And rip apart our wholeness.
They are the potholes that bend
The wheels of progress.

THIS SONG

This song is the foster child of loneliness,
It is the melody no ear heeds.
It calls on the kites,
But they busy themselves
With swoops on chicks
It beckons the eagles,
The comfort of their gliding heights
Separates them from communication.
It telegrams the falcons,
Lo! They are heavenward
With their clawed loots.

This tune is in search listeners,
Yet the trees treasure it
On their leafy ears;
Its echo is hope for tomorrow
This song is the midnight gong
That awakens loot-borne sleeps.
This song is the flies
That gather on carcass.

This refrain is the dreadful hoots of the owl
That sends dread to evil minds.
This voice is the patient vulture
At vigil on the tree top.

This howl is the prayer of the vulture:
Let death spare the elders,
That they counsel the youngsters
That the vulture is not a delicacy
My accent is the fading dusk
Which begets dawn.

THE FATE OF THE COCKROACH

The fate of the cockroach
Resides in the grace that turns
Its back to the shine.
The fate of the cockroach
Are those stamping feet that burst its bowel.
The fate of the cockroach
Is in its sulking death.

The cockroach knows
That the death of one
Sparks off amazing solidarity
From peers in nooks and cranny.

The cockroach rests content in death
Because it knows:
No matter how many entrails are ripped
Peers abound in cupboards
To render unease to the human lot.
The fate of the cockroach
Is the transient life of every being.

So, let no boot, no feet think
They possess the ultimate strength.

THE TEMPEST

The tackling is loosed
The masts are frail
The sails fold inwards
The loot ships nose dive
For there is no anchor to hold the ship
The whirlwind renders vim
To this force.

In vain, they ask for safety
As to the waters they dive.
Let him who knows the bank
Swim to the shore!

The horizon shifts at their approach;
There is no green leaf at sight
No flagging hands, no ahoy
Nor floating debris of life.

The sea depth gleefully summons.
The bellies are full of water;
All powers are diffusing
Limbs shiver at the face of cold
Fingers no more grip pens of fraud
Ague has embraced the big fish
That the sea may know calm.

CONSOLATION

As time beguiles us with abundant hope,
Vain visions crave bright tomorrow
Barren is the insatiability of man.

This landscape, stony, steely, unfathomable
Beclouds witticism and progress.
Hunger, hunger, plague my soul no more!
Deluge of angst and pain flee my being.

Though we bespatter earth on our heads
And sacrifice the joys of our souls;
Though we join the morning birds
And awake dawn with our mourning;
Though we make an ocean
Of our tears and deafen earth
With our grief...
Ash defines mortality
Ordained inevitability is sure to come;
Irrevocable debt must be paid
Surely the sun will set.

VISION

When they rest in time's womb
Lost memories come alive
In moments of reflection.
When deeds are gone,
Present engagements wish rebirth
And ask for eternal youthfulness
In the guise of novel invention.

Vanity is the gift of fate
To barren mortals.

Lost memories recount fairy glories
Of erstwhile calendars
It pray the presence to rewind,
And review the odds of yore,
But such unwholesome request
Is the still birth no maternity delivers.

Fresh phenomena reel the mind future-ward
Reminding the thoughtful man
That existence is the day
Which bears no affinity with night;
A mirage that harbours pains and glory.

Pains of the past,
Glories of the past
Joys of the present,
Fear and fury of the unknown,
Humanity is mere erratic adrenalin.

DREAMS

Here, emotions blazes the high ways of time
Fury, tense, hope, restlessness
Backward, forward, central, oblique, parochial
Clear sighted, myopia, oblivion, melancholy
Fantasy's gift to dreary mind.

In this strange land,
Reality and illusion are mere occupants.
Reality becomes desire and
Transforms to plastic substance.
In dreams, man is made and remade
Formed, reformed and deformed.

In dream, certainty and form are flurry leaves
Under the whims of treacherous wind
Which fan them cold and hot at will.
They know not the place of destiny;
Although they claim life in humans.

Intermittence is the umpire of this game
It separates great nights and day
As it gives life to both.
Dreams erect shaky altars of fortune
And cruelly dissolve same at the face of fruition.
It is the eloquent voice that rebukes
The high excesses of fledgling wishes.

Dream carries the pregnancy of great opposites
And confuse the incomprehensive psyche.
It awakes caution when reality calls.
Like the moments of entertainment,
Which rend your heart at every near miss
Dreams are better interred in time's grave
For man to sleep chaste.

DIVORCE

Rage, reside no more
In this fleshy house.
Affliction, shoo to you!
This body is oiled for immortality.
Worries, I defy your exploit-unwelcome bed fellow
Fear, you are no more in me;
I have known the vanity of possession
My past, present, even future are whole.

I have the art that crafts the wind;
I treasure freedom
And explore wherever at will.

Come forth, come forth!
Stars that guide sages with gifts-
Lead them safely to my abode.

Come forth, come forth!
You mysteries of the philosophers' stone
Which transform alchemy into awesome science.

Come forth, come forth!
You bliss that dwell in the astral realm
Make strong my wings let me glide with you

Come forth, come forth!
You unexplored glory of deep imagination
Mark me as prima facie.

Yet in you all...
I perceive the uniformity of appalling fragrance.
Truly come you heaven made comfort
That defies the treach of gravity;
Take me away beyond mortals,
Where trauma et al are aliens unknown.
Where peace and joy are benign hosts;
Where my heart will be twin to eternal melody
With no more dream
To be neither this nor that.

JUDGEMENT

Yes!
There is an end to every beginning;
Scampering for safety in this no thorough fare
The cross road appears
A cul-de-sac to reckless speed.
Drained of strength,
Malefactors stare blankly.

The owl does not commit sacrilege
Yet it heralds grief to roofs.
The drummers' fingers are frail,
Tunes fade swiftly, feet drag
The hide of the drum is punctured
Echoes of rebirth
Rest in the unattainable tomorrow
Once stomping feet are fatigued
Submission begets modesty.
Like the overfed nza
They've known that obedience to their chi
Is the crucial wisdom.

MY WISH

I resent the palms of pallbearers
I wish no casket to hide this still body,
I wish no tears that will swell lids.
I do not desire to see mourners;
Nor should claques be hired
To display foolery.

I desire not the loneliness of fossilization
In Siberia snowy Alps
Nor the coldness of infirmary morgues.
I yearn not for the hope of the Phoenix
For its essence is resurrection.

I hate to be taken away like Enoch and Elijah
But like Moses, let eyes behold my tomb.
I loathe this human hurly burly,
Purposeful farce: Get gold; get the oil of Arabia,
Let frankincense spiral in the air
Put priceless Gucci and Armani on this body;
Let the coffin be crafted of
Iroko, mahogany, masonia
If possible use the oak or gopher...

Alas...Nothing should make my transition thick.
For all that indulge in these
Mock my exit-for they had wished this stead.

I want to lie still in the virgin jungle
Where no human presence exists,
And extend my charity
To scrambling flies, termites,
Let them eat even to the marrow.
I call forth impatient carrions;
I encourage the insistent worms;
I awake the acute teeth of termites;
For in them, I know the profound sincerity of wickedness
Not the human sham
Where evil adorn tinsels,
Veiling true nature in verbal tales
While subtlety is mummified in spotless bandages
To decoy sights to blindness.

Where the wind that soothes you today
Is the winter that chaps your soul tomorrow
Where your soul die with your spirit
And your body pretend to exist.
I entreat the repose
That will detach me from mortal consequences
Where I will go to my original;
Earth, yours take!

BLACK PEARL

First among equals
I inhabited the holy site of the divine,
Ethiopia knows the root of that Eden River,
Ask Egypt my hindsight,
I sheltered the greatest of kings
And mid-wifed Him in infancy.

This pearl was the pivot of attraction
Modern steel forge is a footnote
Of my ancient invention.

My healing mystery, was the charm
Of all the infirm;
Even the anvil which shapes steels aright
Came from me...
I had abundance to give out
Go, ask Solomon about the largesse
Of my Ethiopian Queen.

But:
I am he whose significant details have diffused
Whose ebony hair have turned scalpy
Whose crystal-clear eye balls of innocence
Are red as they know well
The cruel days of drought and famine

I am he whose loin and matrix
Gave birth and nurtured great males
My females, great heroines of knowledge
I have unexplored packs in my treasure
Waiting to illuminate the dark like fireworks.

I am he whose bowel houses
Gold, bauxite, diamond, crude oil,
But whose fatness is the essence of blown balloon.
I am the black diamond with erstwhile abundance,
My glory no more shines bright;
Answer me you ruthless leaders:
Where is my mystery of mummification?
Where are my craft and wit that made
That only surviving Seven Wonder of ages?
Where is my healing strength of green herbs,
Where is...? Where is...? Where is...?

I am now the monotonous folklore;
Tongues get weary to relate my fairy tales.
My greatness seems fiction
Legendary strength is sterile
Due to the greed of unrepentant prodigals.

My memoir is no more historic
For I have ranged hens
They either peck on my substance
Or scatter with their claws.

I am the rainbow,
My lucid colours are worn,
Nerve-awakening body contours are frail
My afro lies low in weakness
Because they have yielded to strange bedfellows:
Synthetic transplants, cosmetic arsonists, moist dryers.

Barren earth!
I am poached daily
My long tusks, my furly hides, my ivories,
Oh, where are they?
Even my staff of honour, my golden stool
My effigies exist and entertain sights
In glassy cages and shelves;
Great gods, revered deities, life-giving spirits...
Are now impotent and dumb figurines in exhibition
chambers.

Awake from slumber
O sleeping giant,
Loot-prone hands, manglers of essence
Unveil sight, bemoan you flirtation,
Learn from the basking sun,
And dwell no more in your africa.

LUST

Looking into the heart,
One sees the chastity of infancy;
Looking into the mind,
One understands the corruption of adulthood;
Rigid beauty which defies dotage,
Undaunted innocence exposes
The lies of flesh and blood;
Lushness in complexion bloom
Invites sights to its glow.

How in divine thick folds
Those lips gracefully dwell
They bid me to share a kiss,
Spirit and soul bubble, emotions run amok,
Overwhelmed by unexpressed passion.

How in me, desire
Pulls to this elusive display;
Placing ego on the altar of equivocation
As I woo in abstract her part of paradise,
Which in natural form exists.

Moulded in sleek attraction,
These contours dance the tune of distraction
Which have reduced me thus.
This summary of beauty,
Makes the classics toddlers of craft;
Art never imagined this creation.

It strays consciousness to its world
Wherein abides fresh life;
I burn to shake off inhibitions
I aspire to explore wet avenues;
Shivering with zeal to announce feelings,
Reasons sift through my ears, cautions.

Naked, on bent knees, I advance to this altar
But she quietly and cruelly walks away.
Faith, hope of redemption dissolves,
Slowly, dreams fade, reality beckons.

PRAYER

The infirm pray for healing
The undertaker yearns for death to the living
The faithfuls seek the reward of heaven.
As the tyrant covets eternal rein,
The ruled ask for freedom from abuse.

The urchin entreats the benevolence of alms;
The highway thief prays for night to come
As he and its children benefit from its bloom.
The watchman desires dawn
For all acts to be exposed to the sun.

The hopeful fisher poised on his boat
Prays for the derailment of shrewd trout.
The meditative vulture on the tree top in earnest
Seeks the dying man's last breath.
The river calls for both ebb and tide.

The flirtatious female teen for her cycle brood
And loathe motherhood-the token of feminine pride.
The hospital couches beg for sleepers to abide.
The claques delight in letting false tears- for their wages.

It is the dedication of the earthworm's penetrations
That demystifies the earth's depth.
Prayer, the constant elixir of all health;
It desires relief from today`s entanglement
And builds in tomorrow an array of comfort.
Prayer, the weight mankind refuses to offload
As we wear along its road.
Prayer is the nature of the interred grain
Unless it dies, it abides alone.

WHEEL OF FORTUNE

The deceit of youth soothes
With abundant tomorrow;
It hastens today to pass by.

Those who understand its craft
Wake up before dawn;
Knowing creation day is in its cradle,
They make hay while shine endures.

They align the pillars and poles
Allowing no space for laxitude
While the slugs think twilight
Is the glory of continuity.

Old age reminds us of yore days
Either cast in fleeting magnificence
Or marred by the luxuriant youth.
Youth gives us bloated
Hopes that are now stillbirths.

As man sways to his end
The dos, don'ts and never done stare
Stare at our faces.
While the head recounts regrets,
Blood turns hot, the veins weaken,
Heart wanes with unbearable burden
And throbs in counted rhythm.
Flesh and blood are divorced
In their once wholesome state.

MAN

In the image of the divine,
You shine in sublime beauty
In the nature of beasts,
You begrime perfection with act most vile.
You enthrone yourself above all creatures
But lack supposed elation of rank.
In you , is the fierceness of thunder
And the meekness of the dove.

Beasts are proudly beastly
Why can't you be your nature?
You neither ascend to the divine
Nor banish yourself to the adverse.
Lacking the vision of cooperate existence,
You kill and eat others at will;
Yet protect your life with stunning care.

You play almighty to all creatures
But scamper and shudder
When they unleash their anger.

Your heart negates your pride
When I see your adrenaline run mad
At the deeds and sights
Others dare and embrace.
At the forge of mortality,
You bow to inevitability without protest.
The nature of man
Is the strength of vanity.

IT SNOWS

Frostbites persistently attack my palms
Showering flakes turn green fields hoary
Leafless branches moan the treach of winter
Vegetation bears the white burden of ice.

Wrapped human figures,
Scurry and scamper for warmth,
School children huddle together giggling;
Mocking heartily the hooded adults
Whose shivering maturity could not battle cold.

Like wind-flown snows they saunter along,
Hope of life shine bright in their lucid eyes
While the elders cringe at the mystery of continuity
And file their complains about frail joints.
Youths through chattering teeth
Mutter their inaudible tunes
That are neither warm nor cold.

Our marrows have known the pains of time;
For incessant snowy winters
Built memories of gone pains;
Recalled past bears semblance
With our hapless presence
Even our future seems unfathomable.

Like the fallen lizard,
We nod our affirmation to this treachery
Stunned adulthood tries in vain to squash
Under feet the harsh dividends of existence.

The innocence of childhood
Forms promises of laughter
That mimics feeble adulthood.
In childhood, abides genuine heroism
It shrivels worries and diffuses pain
Like the snow that melts away.

It snows; it snows always.
It snows; it snows here and there,
Causing ague and grief for mortals
While the man of childhood
Dares its gory presence
And walks tall in dignity
Making fear a sense of excitement,
An amusing part time.
Knowing that while it snows,
It will surely melt away.

SUICIDE

I go the irreversible way
Not by the crime of any malady
Nor by the treachery of throes,
But by my cherished decision
That myself should be guilty of it;
I should answer for this
So dearly wished
It tells me that if it's worthless,
I should end it.

The world pleases me not
Humans appal me with their falsehood;
Existence, nothing but garden of cactus
Freedom is when selfishness
Puts on the nature of a chameleon
And beguile weak minds to believe its deceit.
Fraternity is mere dream in wasteland
Formed as hangover of a dreary life.
As my neck befriends this noose,
I mock those circumstances that
Hitherto baulked my progress.
As I dangle and wave goodbye to upheavals
I had been folk to.

As I go, I caution every sight
To hold back their waters,
Which never will wash out this deed
But will only expand the gyre of vanity.
Let them cease from their feigned seriousness
Which is the efficacy of nonsense.
Let all who behold me know that
Their void will show
When they meet their cross road.

THE RETURN

The hands of heat has forced
The snail back to its shell;
My cyst seals me from derailment.
In solitude, I am born-again.
Wisdom is my fortitude.

I yearn for translation
But not like the twilight.
Abide with me patience and peace
For in you resides the strength of the spider.
Now, I scale distance like the tortoise
And know my destination before I set off.
I hate the speed which leads to nowhere
Whose hope is in the dusk.

I am coming out as 'lo behold!'
There is no shame of yesterday in me.
My hands have known that duty
Begets abundance and hope.
For my new birth is my vision.

I make no heart mourn me alive
The night in me is now day
It awaits the advancing shine.
In me is the beauty of the dew
With the soothe of its fall.
I bear bright stars
That shoot to vistas beyond reach.
The child of former death has life!

THE WHEEL

Like the fate of
Unfolding rose at sunrise;
Like the emotions of battle-drained soldiers
At the news of armistice.

The wheel,
Like the prisoner
At the tidings of his release;
Like a father
At the return of a prodigal.
Like Nigerians
At the death of Abacha
Like the western world
At the advance of summer
Like a caged bird
At its release to freedom.

The wheel,
Like loving parents keeping vigil at infirmary beds
Like the comatose alone without mobility
Like the sudden burst of explosives
Like the world at the heinous crime of 9/11

The wheel,
Like branches bereft of their leaves
By harsh winter.
Like a range hen
At the sudden swoop of stealthy kite;
Like the condemned criminal
Tied to his stake.
Like a bird at the near miss of a hunter's bullet.
Like the forlorn accused
Pronounced guilty by the judge's hammer;
Like the tethered brutish dog
At the sight of its killers.
Like the blood thirsty gangsters
Doing their macabre dance
Before their prey.

The Wheel,
Like the determined arrow
At the view of its target;
Like the male goat
At the trail of the female.
Like the escort of shadow
At every mobility;
Like the fig tree
At Christ's anger.
Like the suicide
At the abortion of his bid;
Like the vegetable patient
Awaiting the last gasp of life.

The Wheel,
The rotating Wheel,
Like the pregnant tomorrow
With its essence only in our expectations.
Like the revolving globe
Tossing us at will.

THE FAITHFUL

To their synagogue of hate,
Throng them with wishful faces.
Negating the true disciples,
Who with genuine aims squat before the Almighty
And chant vibrant chorus and praises.

They come not to worship the deity of salvation
But to plan and obey their vile desire.
There, the holy man of terror
Extends his sacred hands over all
And mutters his fatal incitation.

Like an unholy aura,
Maniac appetite for death
Engulfs the true humane nature
Pushing to the fore the fiery eyes of evil
Whose sole motive is to make
Mince meat of human bodies
And abandon souls in anguish.

They have filled the hemispheres
With their declarations,
Their blades and steels are
In different races and lives.

Yelling out their fearsome solidarity to aspirants,
Sending weird echoes of evil to the innocent
Who on bent knees and tip toes
Know not what crimes they are preys to.

But when the face of evil shines,
Beings become soulless
Fury besieges the spirit,
Horror untold reigns supreme
As charred debris and mangled steels,
Litter everywhere.

They joy in our grief;
Basking in callous laughter,
Chanting their choruses,
They claim responsibility with clenched fist.

FLOOD

To those distended human bodies
Victims of angry and vengeful nature
I say: you are good testimonies of our mortality!

As I see the glory of lively spirit
Reduced to scattered debris,
When I see great essence of our wellbeing
Dishevelled and cared less for,
I know that order and form
Are mere vanity on plastic plane.

When the great waves of fate pass by,
All most treasured gains, expertise, knowledge, wisdom
Rest dormant in the belly of the sea.
Everywhere, floating corpses grace the face of waters
As humans are humbled to various desolations.

The caged and meticulously watched
Freely roam about in awe;
They, with loneliness are man`s strange allies
The once lord is mastered!

The lion's fierceness is in coma,
Feral hyenas are now mates of timid lambs
Eerie silence has swallowed ferocious howls.
Birds gather consolation in endless hovering,
For there abides no earth for perching.
Consternation unites and defines
The count of misery.

TREACHERY

Distance has truly proved your faithfulness
For out of sight is a strong weapon
For you to frame the schemes of lies.

Being skilled in the act of deception,
You paint the most lucid picture of me,
Expressing falsehood in most affectionate words:
Sweetheart, Sweetie, The love of my life,
While in your secret chambers of truth,
You congratulate your skill and
Mock heartily my derailed emotions.

When you visit your accepted passions,
And relish happiness with them,
Do you still remember deception?
Or is it solely reserved for me?

When you lark with gleeful laughter with them,
When you enjoy their warmth;
When you jerk to the rhythm of their coital push;
When you moan and groan at their expertise at it;
The same amorous names you call Tom is for Dick and
Harry
Aarh! What a generosity!

Well, the voice of chemistry is non-variance
In all experiment laboratories
For blood must yield to the sense affection
Expressed in gentle touches and caresses.

When this act you cherish much is done
You come out with transient regrets
Why did I do it?
I shouldn't have done it
Why didn't I resist it?
But will he know?
After all he is away
And my deception binds him firm.
Well it is done and will be done again.

These your rhetorics of vanity
Are the gains of a wasteful love.
Well, farewell falsehood and all that mould you!

GLOSSARY

Okpoko . . . . a quaking bird of prey

Almageris. . . . . . . the dejected teenagers of Northern Nigeria

Ibi . . . . disease of the scrotum that leaves it swollen

Nza . . . . a wren

Agbada

Asoke

Abada. . . . . local textiles native to Africa

Gidigwom . . . . . . sudden huge bang

Chi. . . . . personal god. Believed to determine an individual's destiny

Abacha. . . . . Nigeria's military dictator

Maroko . . . . erstwhile notorious slum in Nigeria